The Walk

Carla Bastos

"The Walk," by Carla Bastos. ISBN 978-1-60264-417-5.

Published 2009 by Virtualbookworm.com Publishing Inc., P.O. Box 9949, College Station, TX 77842, US. ©2009, Carla Bastos. All rights reserved. No part of this publication may be reproduced, stored in a retrieval system, or transmitted in any form or by any means, electronic, mechanical, recording or otherwise, without the prior written permission of Carla Bastos.

Manufactured in the United States of America.

To Zoe and Troy

Also by Carla Bastos:

A Steadfast Spirit

Loving

Introduction

Early in my Christian walk I was encouraged to apply the J-O-Y (Jesus, Others, You) concept for a successful life in Christ. It all sounded pretty simple: If we'll just put Jesus first in worship, fellowship and obedience, then esteem others higher than ourselves and, finally, position our own issues last in the mix, then we'll be pleasing to God and find inner joy in the process.

But, let's be honest. It's a pretty tough proposition. There's this old fallen world, this sinful flesh and, just when we think we've conquered them, there's the devil faithfully working to foil the whole plan. After all, let's face it – stuff happens. Life is not a cakewalk.

So, rather than just professing our Christianity and then walking it out as best we can, maybe there's more we can do. Maybe by breaking the whole thing down into bite-sized chunks and being a little more proactive about this Christian walk, we can achieve better success. And, who knows, we may even find that ever-elusive joy in the process.

Let's start with a radical approach (I grew up in the sixties). Let's reverse the process and see what it takes to walk out our Christianity with ourselves first. After all, for many of us, self is our biggest obstacle. If we can learn to put up with ourselves, we'll see where The Walk takes us from there…

1.

Walking With Self

Carla Bastos

As You Love Yourself

Sure, it's a touchy subject. Many Christians find that it's a thin line, a dangerous, slippery slope to negotiate – loving oneself while not being selfish or self-centered.

While the super-spiritual among us may not want to admit it, we are already big-time lovers of self. And that's not a bad thing. Yes, the Word says that men will be lovers of self in the evil last days (2 Tim. 3:2). And I do believe we are living in those days. But, there is a way in which God intends for us to love ourselves.

Consider how much time and expense we devote to the upkeep of both our inner and outer selves. Every visit to the doctor, every haircut or manicure, every time we pop a vitamin or strap on a seatbelt, says we love ourselves and are committed to our own safety, maintenance and preservation. And, there's an even stronger indication.

> *For, where your treasure is,*
> *there your heart will be also.*
> *Matt. 6:21*

Like it or not, our pocketbooks speak the loudest of all. The reason store shelves are lined with hundred-dollar anti-aging creams and vitamin supplements is because retailers know we'll buy them. (Sadly, although Americans are the biggest producers and consumers of health products, we are still the unhealthiest country on the planet. Seems we'd rather just go ahead and have that double cheeseburger, and then spend a fortune for a diet plan or gym membership – which we won't use!)

Whatever our preferred poison and follow-up remedy, the fact is, whenever we spend our hard-earned cash on ourselves, it's because we love ourselves. And, while we may have God's original intent a little blurred and confused at times, He does indeed want us to love ourselves. After all, He told us to love others *as* we love ourselves.

Carla Bastos

Caring for the outer self and the physical body comes easier to most of us than managing the inner spiritual and psychological self. This is where the rubber meets the road – where walking with self becomes tricky. If you're the analytical, introspective type (like some of us, who shall go nameless), this stuff can make you a little crazy.

Take the ongoing struggle with sin, for example. And yes, it is ongoing for all of us. Anyone who tells you they've "arrived" is being disingenuous. But, the struggle is different for each of us. Not only does one person have different weaknesses than another, but each may have a unique approach to dealing with those weaknesses. One person will fast, another will seek counsel or perhaps use a self-help program. Still another just beats himself up mercilessly every time the struggle surfaces – which, by the way, is never the answer.

Often our greatest struggles are in areas that we don't want to discuss with friends or counselors. In fact, one of the reasons we're so hard on ourselves is that we tend to believe we're the only one fighting this battle. How mortified we'd be if anyone knew!

There are also issues that God *wants* us to walk out alone. Think about it: Not only did He create us to be unique individuals, but He also placed a unique calling on each of our lives. Our preparation to fulfill that calling may be a very private, lonely journey.

The good news is, even though we may have to walk a certain road alone, the road itself has been well-traveled. And those roads are many. It's okay if we choose a different route to get to the same destination, so long as we stay on the course God designed for us – and us alone.

Walking successfully with self means not mimicking someone else's method of dealing with their sins or problems. Let the Lord show you the personal path He's designed for you. Then, the key is to stay on that path, to press on, to continue in the pursuit of perfection. Will you achieve it on this earth? No, but God knows that. He knows our frame, and remembers that we are dust (Psalm 103:14). That's why He's given us each a road on which to travel:

A highway shall be there, and a road. And it shall be called the Highway of Holiness. The unclean shall not pass over it, but it shall be for others. Whoever walks the road, although a fool, shall not go astray. No lion shall be there, nor shall any ravenous beast go up on it; it shall not be found there. But the redeemed shall walk there.

Isaiah 35:8-9

Beyond the sin aspect of our walk with self, there is the matter of dealing with our own quirks and idiosyncrasies. We have to live and work with other people from day to day, so these ways of ours have to be reconciled with our walk with others. But, the first step to that end is dealing with our own habits and mannerisms.

This may be one of those areas where we don't find a lot of self-love. We develop habits and methods of doing things, and then become set in those ways, often without even realizing it. We don't know how or why we became the way we are and, even if we don't like these things in ourselves, we often feel powerless to change them.

This is where it is helpful to remember two important things: (1) God made us, and He doesn't make mistakes. Whatever character traits we've developed, they are not a surprise to Him; (2) If something needs changing, He is well able to walk us through the process.

There was a time in my life when I'd developed habits of fastidiousness and perfectionism that were beginning to control my lifestyle and interfere with my relationships. Although I was unable to overcome these tendencies alone, God had a solution. He called me to full-time missions work, taking away the control and the need for perfect order to which I was becoming addicted. (In the process of resolving these issues, the Lord also reaffirmed His grand sense of humor that we've all come to know and love.)

Once again, the key here is to embrace our God-given individuality, and not be too hard on ourselves for the attributes that make us who we are.

Consider also your environment. There's an age-old "which came first" debate as to whether or not we are actually products of our environment. That question won't be answered here, but there can be no doubt that our home environment certainly affects who we are and how we behave. The same is true in every country and culture. I've known people who were ashamed of their background, their family or their accent, and worked hard to leave the past behind and re-invent themselves. But, once again, God knew where and into what family or people group we would be born, before we were ever conceived. None of our cultural norms, habits or idiosyncrasies is surprising to our Creator, and we can be sure that He had a good reason for ordaining or allowing each one. Rather than being intent on changing or hiding the things that make us who we are, perhaps we should see what the Lord has to say about it. No doubt He would have us glean the good and get rid of the bad. You know – eat the meat and spit out the bones.

When contemplating our walk with self, it's important to remember who is in control. It's not sinful to love oneself, and it's not ungodly to consider our own well-being and desires during life's journey. If our priority is to seek the heart and will of God, then we can rest in the knowledge of several key truths:

- God loves me more than I love me.

- He will give me the desires of my heart, and remove those desires that are not in accordance with His will or in my best interest.

- He is in control. If I'm sold out and surrendered to Him, then I need not be afraid of walking in the light, just myself and my Lord. My love for self will be healthy and balanced, and will bring glory to Him, – and He will grant me His rest and His peace. Just as my love for self is not of the worldly variety, so also is the peace He gives me – not as the world gives.

As we consider God's hand in our lives and reach this place of serenity and security, we become stronger and more confident. We're now able to receive and reciprocate God's love, and we're starting our walk with sure footing on solid ground. But, now it's time to step outside the front door.

Straight Paths

One of the most troublesome areas in our walk with self is – well, self. Life's tough, so it's hard to say why we insist on making it so much more difficult than it already is. But, the fact remains that if an annoying neighbor, a pesky co-worker, an impatient driver, or Satan himself won't sabotage things in our lives, then we stand ready to step in and do the job for them.

Of course, there are those who thrive on strife, confusion and chaos. But, what about the rest of us? We may be regular folks leading run-of-the-mill lives, but what about some of those goofy decisions we make, and then the stubbornness that causes us to dig in our heels and refuse to undo the damage? Even those who aren't drama queens or kings are given to the occasional shot in the foot.

The Walk

Those who may have an otherwise stellar Christian walk can succumb to the bitterness and resentment that makes us cut off our nose to spite our face.

So, why do we do it? And, how do we stop? As with many things in life, the key here may just be a little planning. If you're not a list-maker or a control freak, trying to plan out too many areas of your life may sound a bit like legalistic bondage. But, hear me out. It's a concept that is doable for us all, and may actually give us more freedom and control over some of the dumb things we find ourselves doing in this walk with self.

> *Therefore, strengthen the hands which hang down, and the feeble knees, and make straight paths for your feet, so that what is lame may not be dislocated, but rather be healed.*
>
> *Pursue peace with all people, and holiness, without which no one will see the Lord; looking carefully lest anyone fall short of the grace of God; lest any root of bitterness springing up cause trouble,*

and by this many become defiled.
Hebrews 12:12-15

Making straight paths for ourselves is a choice that we can make daily. But many of us choose to hobble along on the crooked, craggy paths of life, making minimal progress and wearing ourselves out in the process.

Suppose you find yourself in a bad financial situation, maybe credit card debt or some other unmet obligation. You have a couple of options here. You can throw a pity party, decide that you deserve a break from the stress of it all, and go out and charge a few new outfits or a weekend getaway. After all, what's a few more dollars, when you already owe thousands?

That, of course, would be making a crooked path for yourself, one whose end may take you twice as long to reach.

Say you have a fight with your spouse and, rather than work toward resolution, you decide this is the opportune time to bring up everything he or she has ever done wrong since the dawn of time. May as well add a little fire to the mix, right?

Another crooked path.

Granted, making straight paths takes discipline, and we won't always get it right. Temptation is a powerful thing – that desire to splurge on material things or to prove ourselves right in an argument. But, we can work toward mastering those temptations and making straight paths for our lives. Remember, we're talking about walking with self. If we're going to be able to stand ourselves at all, then we'll simply have to get a firm grip in these areas and learn how to control our lives, rather than letting our lives control us.

I believe one of the most important words in the English language is *balance,* and sometimes we must glance at the scales before we leap. If we'll choose a game plan of weighing our decisions and counting the cost before going forward, our paths will be much straighter and easier to navigate.

Soul Control

Our Christian walk is not rocket science. In fact, for those of us who may be a little dense or hard of hearing, we are given repeated instruction throughout the Bible:

> *He has shown you, O man, what is good; and what does the Lord require of you but to do justly, to love mercy, and to walk humbly with your God?*
>
> *Micah 6:8*

> *For this is the love of God, that we keep His commandments. And His commandments are not burdensome.*
>
> *1 John 5:3*

> *I say then: Walk in the Spirit, and you shall not fulfill the lust of the flesh.*
>
> *Gal. 5:16*

Of all the fruits of the Spirit listed in Galatians 22, self-control may be the least sought-after. But, when it comes to our Christian walk with self, with others and with God, self-control is essential. It will keep us from impulsive, rash decisions, and from being quick to speak and slow to listen – you know, the old proverbial foot-in-mouth dilemma.

Self-control and discipline are also symbolic of maturity in our walk. In order to grow and progress, to be useful to the Lord and prepared for ministry, we must diligently seek the spiritual fruit of self-control. Note the Apostle Paul's references to discipline and control in counseling his spiritual son Titus in the work of appointing elders in the church:

> *For a bishop must be blameless, as a steward of God, not self-willed, not quick-tempered, not given to wine, not violent, not greedy for money, but hospitable, a lover of what is good, sober-minded, just, holy, self-controlled.*
> *Titus 1:7-8*

The soul is defined by many as the combination of mind, will and emotions. In other words, those elements of our humanness that are up to us – and therefore hardest to control. Man has struggled with his soul since the beginning of time.

Consider David, who on the one hand demonstrated complete control of his soul:

*My soul shall make its boast in the Lord...
My soul shall be joyful in the Lord;*

yet, at other times showed frustration at his own lack of control:

For my soul is full of troubles... Why are you cast down, O my soul?

Even though David fought the same battles you and I fight every day for control of the soul, he knew wherein lay the victory. He understood that, while we are charged with self-control, it is our Creator who is ultimately in control of us, and we must daily surrender that control to Him. Our responsibility is first to lean on those great, everlasting arms; then, to strive to walk in discipline, obedience and patience – both with ourselves and with the Holy Spirit working in us. Only as we begin to grow in these areas of our walk will we be able to stay on the straight paths of peace, humility and joy that enable us to walk with – and tolerate – self.

*By your patience possess your souls.
Luke 21.19*

Together, Alone

Walking the Christian walk alone inherently involves others. Sounds oxymoronic, doesn't it? But, a major factor in determining who we will become in Christ, and how His Word and His ways will manifest in us, includes determining how we will conduct ourselves in relationships.

Life is all about relationships, and they are an integral part of who God wants each of us to be as individuals. Learning to relate to others in an acceptable way is, for many, a lifelong pursuit. But, we all have the same roadmap, and if we'll just stay on course, we'll get there. Some of us just choose the scenic route.

There is only one true God, and His Word applies to all of us. For example, the Great Commission is given to everyone who professes Jesus Christ as Lord and Savior. We are all to obey it. But, not everyone is called to be a missionary or an evangelist. And, even among the ranks of missionaries, some focus on evangelism, some on teaching, others on translation, medicine, etc.

Take marriage as another example. We are under a scriptural mandate that the husband is the head of the wife. Some couples take this to mean the husband makes all the decisions pertaining to family, finances, etc. Others work together in these matters, with the husband serving as his wife's covering.

Of course, this doesn't mean we get to take license with "gray" areas in Scripture, or choose to apply them willy-nilly. Thou shalt not kill, steal, lie, commit adultery, etc. Period. Any subjectivity in walking out the Word can only enter into the mix when we understand that, although we are individuals, and we're all different in our gifts, talents, etc., our God-given individuality carries with it the obligation of maturity, responsibility and obedience to God's Word.

The Walk

Some are morning people while others are night owls. Some are readers, others drawn to audio or video media. God made us that way. Couples must know His word and then know and understand themselves and one another before they can determine how God wants His mandates applied in their own lives.

The same is true of individuals. By Jesus' example, and throughout the Bible, we are taught to be defenders of the defenseless, helpers of the helpless. But, does that mean I should take up arms and take to the streets in a vigilante's campaign? Run for office and join the ranks of lawmakers? Or, stay home and commit my life to prayer and fasting on behalf of the poor and oppressed?

Well, I happen to feel more comfortable writing letters to those lawmakers, or editorials to newspapers, in defense of the defenseless. For several years of my life, I applied this area of the Word in a more hands-on fashion, on the mission field. And, still today, I make prayer and fasting on behalf of others a priority. If pursued with a pure heart, as unto the Lord, any and all of these applications of the scriptural directive can be considered walking in obedience. (However, I strongly advise against that whole vigilante thing.)

Imagine having a dear friend who has a particular need – for emotional support, financial help, whatever the case may be. How and to what degree you step up to help your friend is going to be determined by your lone walk with self and with the Lord. Say this person has a need for $1000. Someone may be compelled to lend $500 out of their abundance, expecting it to be returned when their friend is able. Someone else may give the full $1000 sacrificially, and never expect repayment. Neither is necessarily wrong.

Likewise, there are those of us who are comfortable holding someone's hand, listening, counseling or crying together. Others would rather make a meal or clean the house – something more practical.

There are employees who are borderline slackers. They may do their jobs thoroughly and well, but rarely go the extra mile for anyone or anything. Others consistently go above and beyond. Both are walking in obedience (sort of).

The Walk

These are all examples of how our relationships and interactions with others are inextricably linked to our walk with self. The key here is to truly know oneself, which I believe few of us really do. Who you really are deep down, that persona that was developed and honed in your personal, private walk with God and with yourself, is the single determining factor in your relationships with others. And, in case you're not sure what you're really made of, just observing how you respond to others can be quite revealing.

Years ago, Charles Colson and Nancy Pearcey wrote a book called, *How Now Shall We Live?* I absolutely loved the premise. I summed it up as a call for each of us to determine who and what we will be in this life, and then simply be that. Just do it. Not by rote, or in a mechanical or obligatory fashion. Not because Pastor or Oprah said so, or because everyone else is doing it. Rather, because we are fearfully and wonderfully made, with gifts and talents and individuality. We are vibrant, complex creatures, each as vital to the big picture as the other. And, once we know and understand and begin to walk out that special self that God created us to be, we become a vital part of a family, a group, a church, a society – strategically placed exactly where He wants us, making our own important contribution, in intimate communion with Himself, each day becoming more comfortable in our own skin, growing in our walk with self and in relationship with others.

O Lord, You have searched me and known me. You know my sitting down and my rising up; You understand my thought afar off. You comprehend my path and my lying down, and are acquainted with all my ways.
For there is not a word on my tongue, but behold, O Lord, You know it altogether. You have hedged me behind and before, and laid Your hand upon me.
Such knowledge is too wonderful for me; it is high, I cannot attain it. Where can I go from Your Spirit? Or where can I flee from your presence? If I ascend into heaven, You are there; if I make my bed in hell, behold, You are there. If I take the wings of the morning, and dwell in the uttermost parts of the sea, even there Your hand shall lead me, and Your right hand shall hold me. If I say, "Surely the darkness shall fall on me," even the night shall be light about me; indeed, the darkness shall not hide from You, but the night shines as

The Walk

the day; the darkness and the light are both alike to You. For You formed my inward parts; You covered me in my mother's womb. I will praise You, for I am fearfully and wonderfully made; marvelous are Your works, and that my soul knows very well. My frame was not hidden from You, when I was made in secret, and skillfully wrought in the lowest parts of the earth. Your eyes saw my substance, being yet unformed. And in Your book they all were written, the days fashioned for me, when as yet there were none of them. How precious also are Your thoughts to me, O God! How great is the sum of them! If I should count them, they would be more in number than the sand; When I awake, I am still with You.

Psalm 139:1-18

II.

Walking With Others

Playing Well With Others

Do you remember grade school, when your report card contained a section entitled, *Plays Well With Others?* Well, I didn't. Oh, I wasn't a troublemaker or a bully or anything. Quite the opposite.

Like many "misfits" in school (and sometimes, throughout life), I was a bit of a geek, a nerd. Getting straight A's every year, and coming from a strict, religious home that precluded much hanging out with the other kids made me plenty unpopular. But, the funny thing was, I didn't care much for popularity. I didn't *want* to hang out. I just didn't play well with others.

Fortunately, I eventually learned that it was okay not to fit in. In fact, I found that there were many other misfits out there, and we each had something special to contribute. While I never became the most social of creatures, I figured out how to give and receive love, and to enjoy social interactions.

For many people, finding good in others, interacting with them and being a caring friend and listener, are all learned behaviors. Those with more private, reclusive personalities must make a conscious effort to become more social. But, it's an important part of our Christian walk, and an effort we must make. We were made to be social creatures.

Understanding these truths means understanding that social interaction is not optional. I've known Christians over the years who proudly proclaimed that they "fly solo" or "worship in their own way." Translation? They don't go to church. Others purposely attend a mega-church so that they can remain anonymous, with no ministerial obligations or pressure to get to know anyone outside of church.

Sadly, these solitary souls have missed the point. They have a faulty understanding of fellowship, and only a partial picture of church membership and all that it entails.

> *A mom woke her son up for church one Sunday morning, but he refused. "I don't want to go to that church," he whined. "I don't like those people and they don't like me. Give me three reasons why I should go there!"*
>
> *"Well," his mother answered calmly, "because I'm your mother and I said so; because you're 35 years old; and, because you're the pastor."*

Okay, that scenario might be a little far-fetched. But, when you think about it, many people attend church grudgingly, or as some obligatory weekly ritual that they're forced to endure. Maybe it's a new church where they haven't made friends and don't yet feel comfortable; maybe the church is too large or too small, the worship is too loud or the pastor is too boring. (Or, could it be that those sermons are like sandpaper, and the Holy Spirit is just too convicting?) Whatever the excuses, we must forge past them.

The Walk

There are proactive measures that we can take to change such wrong thinking about church membership:

a) Make a list of all the things we can give *and* receive from regular church attendance;

b) Purposely change our expectations, basing them not on rumor or past experience, but choosing to believe and expect the best.

These two simple steps can be applied to every area of our Christian walk (and life itself) that calls for playing well with others.

Have you heard the old story of two families who both relocated from the same old town to the same new one? When asked by their new neighbors how things were in the old town, the Joneses said, "The people were unfriendly and we didn't get along with any of them." But the Smiths said, "We made a lot of wonderful friends and we really loved living there." Interestingly, when asked by the old neighbors how they liked their new town, both families' answers were still the same! The difference in these families' viewpoints? Expectations. One family expected to find good people wherever they went, and obviously made the effort to seek them out. The other family simply didn't expect to find friends – and they didn't.

One of the wrong methods we use to form expectations is thinking only of self. *How will this affect me? What will they think of me? What's in it for me?* When we think this way, we're effectively saying, *It's all about me. Nothing else matters.* If you think it's all about you, and I think it's all about me, we'll find ourselves at an impasse, unable to play well together. And, we'll both be shortchanged in the process.

All of our earthly relationships are give-and-take. But, none can thrive if there's too much giving or taking. There are those who will suck the life out of us if we let them, and it is our responsibility to prevent that from happening by setting boundaries. Healthy relationships are balanced relationships, and it is to our mutual advantage to nurture these connections.

I'm often intrigued by the Old Testament relationship between David and

The Walk

Jonathan. While there are many lessons we can take from their model, one example is particularly striking. As David fled Jonathan's father, Saul, in fear of his very life, Jonathan came to David to encourage him in the Lord:

> *Then Jonathan, Saul's son, arose and went to David in the woods and strengthened his hand in God. And he said to him, "Do not fear, for the hand of Saul my father shall not find you. You shall be king over Israel, and I shall be next to you. Even my father Saul knows that."*
> *1 Samuel 23:16-17*

Later, when David's own people rose up against him, he was able to strengthen himself in the Lord – no doubt because Jonathan had made the time and effort to take those early steps with him.

> *Now David was greatly distressed, for the people spoke of stoning him, because the soul of all the people was grieved, every man for his sons and his daughters. But David*

> *strengthened himself in the Lord his God.*
>
> *1 Samuel 30:6*

Have you ever noticed a new believer, or even a long-time church member, struggling to find peace or encouragement to get through a tough situation? These are the times that are most important in our walk together with others. It may be just a small gesture of friendship, or possibly a greater effort like Jonathan's that is required. In either case, if we will step up to meet that need, we can be assured that our encouragement will bear good fruit.

Intercession – The Abigail Way

For all of our Christian grandiosity, it's amazing what accomplished bystanders some have turned out to be. It's as if we've taken courses in not getting involved, and worked our whole lives to perfect the practice. By now, some are professional bystanders, maybe even in the running for the Bystander CEO post.

But, playing well with others inherently means getting involved with others. Getting involved with others means

The Walk

caring enough to intercede on their behalf. The operative term here is *caring.* This is important because, even though intercession will gain great rewards for the intercessor, both on earth and in heaven, that must not be our motive. It's sort of like tithing – we do so because we love the Lord and want to obey His mandate, not because of the return we're expecting on our investment.

When we think of intercession, we often think of prayer, which is usually the most available and effective form. However, there are times when action is required. In order to know whether to act and how to proceed, we must *already* be keenly in tune with the Holy Spirit.

When David and his small army were on the run from Saul, they depended on the kindness of strangers for sustenance. At one point they came to the house of Nabal, a very rich man whose servants had previously been helped by David and his men. David had paid it forward, and all he now sought from Nabal was a return of that favor – the give-and-take that we depend on in our walk with others. But Nabal refused to share his food and water, prompting David to plan an attack against him. Enter Abigail.

Then Abigail made haste and took two hundred loaves of bread, two skins of wine, five sheep already dressed, five seahs of roasted grain, one hundred clusters of raisins, and two hundred cakes of figs, and loaded them on donkeys. And she said to her servants, "Go on before me; see, I am coming after you." But she did not tell her husband Nabal. So it was, as she rode on the donkey, that she went down under cover of the hill; and there were David and his men, coming down toward her, and she met them.

Now when Abigail saw David, she dismounted quickly from the donkey, fell on her face before David, and bowed down to the ground. So she fell at his feet and said: "On me, my lord, on me let this iniquity be! And please let your maidservant speak in your ears, and hear the words of your maidservant. Please, let not my lord regard this scoundrel Nabal. For as his name is, so is he: Nabal is his name, and folly is with him! But I, your maidservant, did not see the young men of my lord whom you sent.

Now therefore, my lord, as the Lord lives and as your soul lives, since the Lord has held you back from coming to bloodshed and from avenging yourself with your own hand, now then, let your enemies and those who seek harm for my lord be as Nabal. And now this present which your maidservant has brought to my lord, let it be given to the young men who follow my lord. Please forgive the trespass of your maidservant. For the Lord will certainly make for my lord an enduring house, because my lord fights the battles of the Lord, and evil is not found in you throughout your days.
1 Samuel 25:18-20, 23-28

Abigail's intercessory tools had clearly been sharpened in a long-standing, intimate relationship with the Lord. They included:

- Wisdom. Prior verses state that Abigail was a woman of understanding. She not only had the God-given discernment to know that David was headed for the throne, but she understood that she had been given a role in the process.
- Timing. Notice that, as soon as she learned of the situation, Abigail *made haste* to spring into action. But, this was not an impulsive decision on her part. She had certainly spent considerable time on her knees, preparing for this very moment.
- Humility. The deference Abigail showed to David was not only part of her beauty, but an important part of the effectiveness of her intercession.

Abigail's motives in intercession were threefold: to protect Nabal from David's vengeance, leaving his punishment to God and God alone; to protect David from acting rashly, thereby obstructing his path to the throne; and, to protect herself from any fallout in the matter. Her preparation, motives and actions in intercession are an excellent model for us today as we consider our intercessory role in our walk with others.

Whether in intercession, church fellowship, a recreational setting or individual friendships, the same concept applies: Give a little, take a little. Why not take a step of faith and be the first to give a little? A smile, a compliment, a lunch invitation – or even focused intercession on behalf of someone in need. It may be outside our comfort zone, but this is how we learn to play well with others.

God has designated a church home and rewarding relationships for each one of His children. These are the body of Christ, His family. His Word says that He sets the solitary in families (Ps. 68:6). And it is His will that we walk this walk – and play well – together.

Small Groups

The small group phenomenon is enjoying increasing popularity today, but its origins are actually found in the early church:

> *And they continued steadfastly in the apostles' doctrine and fellowship, in the breaking of bread, and in prayers.*
>
> *So, continuing daily with one accord in the temple, and breaking bread from house to house, they ate their food with gladness and simplicity of heart.*
>
> Acts 2:42, 46

Small groups are centered around the concept of fellowship, a bedrock principle in Christianity. Defined as *compan-*

ionship, friendliness, communion between persons having similar tastes, interests, etc., the concept of fellowship is a necessary element of mutual support and encouragement. These were key in the persecuted early church, and they are key today. Once we've gained the self-awareness and control that allows us to know God's will for our lives and develop a healthy, confident Christian walk, then we must put those attributes to work in lifting up and encouraging others.

Of course, churches and ministries have widely varying ideas of what a small group should look like, and that's a good thing. I've observed small group ministries that were based on parishioners' neighborhood proximity to one another, and others that involved all groups meeting at the same time on the same day (in replacement of the church's Sunday evening service), and studying the same prepared lesson. Most small groups these days are probably based on mutual interests and are held on a date and time convenient for all members. There are men's groups, women's groups, football or bowling groups, book clubs, and more.

In the text, *Competent Christian Counseling* by Drs. Timothy Clinton and George Ohlschlager, the importance and the various goals of small groups are discussed:

> 1. *Task groups exist to accomplish a certain project (such as organizing a retreat, selecting furniture, planning a service).*
>
> 2. *Teaching groups communicate knowledge and information largely through the lecture method of discussion (as in Sunday school classes and educational programs).*
>
> 3. *Growth groups encourage and challenge members in areas such as marriage, family and work life, Bible mastery, discipleship, self-esteem, codependency, community outreach, or social justice.*
>
> 4. *Support groups, offered by progressive churches, focus on specific emotional or relational needs. Generally, members attend because they feel stress in coping with life's problems. People need support and perspective in dealing with issues*

such as job loss, marriage breakup, single parenting and codependency.

Although the Christian counseling community agrees that small groups are essential to the good health of the body of Christ, it should be noted that laypersons are not qualified counselors. Our ministry to one another through small groups is borne of the cohesiveness and bonds that are established.

No matter the purpose or format, the common threads woven throughout the small group phenomenon are a scriptural foundation, shared beliefs, and a fellowship that allows members to be comfortable in their Christianity, and to support and encourage one another.

The comfort factor is important. How often do we find churchgoers donning a "happy mask" on Sunday, only to go home and fight with the spouse, yell at the children, kick the dog and dread going to work on Monday morning? Once we spend time with others outside of church, we learn that we're not alone. Everyone has a happy mask, and no one seems to think anyone else is as big a sinner as he or she. In an informal setting we can feel more comfortable letting our hair down, taking off the mask and maybe even sharing counsel and prayer for the issues of life.

One element of the small group that seems to be universal is the breaking of bread together. The old concept of "food, fun and fellowship" still holds true in Christian gatherings today (thank God!) This biblical standard may have indeed been borne of the all-important comfort factor. Eating in most societies is a social event. Along with the recreational pursuits common to many small groups, it promotes the notion that our Christian walk is a 24-7 undertaking. It is not a Sunday morning/Wednesday night proposition, but it is *who we are.*

Go back to the early church for a moment. These hearty souls did not just show up for twice-weekly church meetings and then leave their Christianity in the sanctuary. They *lived* Jesus Christ. They understood that their Christian witness and brotherhood with one another were the core of their being. Consider the persecution and dispersion of Christians which, by all accounts and expectations, should have brought an end to the church altogether. But it didn't.

The Walk

Contrary to what many may believe, the world was not "turned upside down" by the apostles only, because they stayed in Jerusalem for the most part. Regular, everyday folks -- fishermen, tentmakers, housewives and carpenters – spoke of Jesus as they carried water from the well, drew fish in the sand with their toe as they met along the way, and gathered in one another's homes to pray and break bread. Their Christian walk was not an occasional clock-punching event. It was their life. The small group lends itself to carrying on this tradition.

While some small groups may be designed strictly to share recreational interests, mutual support and encouragement can still play a key role. Scripture tells us to confess our sins to one another (James 5:16). Of course, this doesn't mean we have to air every stitch of our dirty laundry for all the world to see. In fact, there are those who steer clear of small groups because they dread just such an ordeal. Their concerns are valid. It is crucially important that these gatherings don't turn into gossip-fests. However, if not abused, small groups can be a great opportunity to take off the mask and make the connections we all need.

A successful walk with others involves holding up one another's arms when necessary, rejoicing with those who rejoice and weeping with those who weep. With care, the small group environment provides fertile soil for growing new relationships and sharing day-to-day trials and prayer requests – all-important ingredients in this area of our Christian walk.

Body Bags and Graveclothes

No, our walk together is not a funeral march. There's plenty of life to be found in these connections, but nurturing and revival may be in order. Just as our walk with the Lord is refreshed after a season of fasting or a new Bible study, and our marital relationships are made new with counseling or a romantic getaway, so, too can our walk with others be revived.

Perhaps a different vantage point will give us fresh perspective, maybe even help us to see our Christian walk with others as God sees it.

The Body's Baggage

Air travel has changed drastically since September 11th. We're warned constantly against carrying the bags of someone we don't know, or letting a stranger carry our bags. Anything can happen. We might find ourselves taking responsibility for things we don't want, and have no business with anyway. Or, someone may offer to help with our luggage only to abscond with the things we hold dear.

We would do well to heed those same warnings in our journey through life. Everybody's got baggage. But, it's *their* baggage, and ours is ours. Sure, we'd like to be good Christians and do a good deed and help someone out with their baggage. And, we certainly wouldn't want to insult anyone by not accepting their offer to help with our bags. But, as mentioned earlier, we must strike a balance. And we must employ wisdom.

> *But may the God of all grace, who called us to His eternal glory by Christ Jesus, after you have suffered a while, perfect, establish, strengthen, and settle you.*
> 1 Peter 5:10

Knowing when it's appropriate to help someone in the body of Christ with their baggage requires keen discernment. There are times when the Lord allows His children to suffer, and it is He, and He alone, who will comfort us and relieve our suffering.

Helping others with their baggage can be likened to rushing to the aid of our own children when they cry out for our help. From the smallest infants, children are sometimes allowed to cry for awhile, to figure out their own solution, or to finally give in and obey what their parents have been saying all along. Only then will they be comforted. Similarly, if we're irresponsible with money, for example, God wouldn't want our friends to step in and bail us out every time we're in a bind. His Word says if anyone will not work, neither shall he eat (2 Thess. 3:10), so we have no business sneaking a snack to someone who is in rebellion. In other words, as our loving parent, God would rather we suffer a while, in order that we can be perfected, established, strengthened and settled.

There are times when we don't understand God's reason for allowing suffering, either in our own lives or in the lives of others. This lack of understanding is an even more compelling reason not to step in and perhaps foil God's plan in someone's life. We often don't have enough information to see the big picture, usually because the matter is between the Lord and His child – and no business of ours.

Have you ever noticed how children will appeal to grandparents for sympathy after being disciplined by parents? We tend to do that with one another. If God is disciplining us, or simply desiring to teach or grow us in a particular area, we'll often appeal to another member of the body rather than hear and obey what the Father is saying. We don't want to endure suffering. But, there's danger in trying to carry one another's baggage. You may be so busy dealing with my issues that the devil is having a field day with yours.

Each member of the body of Christ must carry his or her own bags. It is the only way any of us will eventually be relieved of these burdens. We must hear what the Father is saying, whether He's telling us it's time to step in and help, or to keep our hands off. Most importantly, we must obey, whether we're the one doing the suffering or the one trying to help.

Loose Them

Graveclothes are described in Christian circles as the wrappings that bind us to the things of the world and of the flesh. In other words, although we are born again, we often live our lives as though we are dead, still trapped in the vanities of our sinful lives. And, unlike the baggage that the body of Christ often *chooses* to hold onto, graveclothes keep us bound and unable to break free even if we wanted to. That's where our ministry to one another comes in.

While pondering the raising of Lazarus from the dead, I've often been curious about the method and sequence Jesus employed. Although He simply spoke resurrection life into Lazarus, the Lord left him bound in his graveclothes and commanded others to loose him. What was up with *that?*

Just as Jesus used different methods of healing in different situations – according to the deeper, spiritual need of the one being healed – so also did He have a strategic purpose in the lives of Lazarus and the surrounding witnesses. Sure, He could have just as easily commanded the graveclothes to supernaturally fall from the man's body. But, we serve an efficient God. He is not one to waste a miracle or let a teachable moment slip by.

Jesus' first objective in this miracle was to glorify God and to show the witnesses that He was sent by the Father:

> *Jesus said to her, "Did I not say to you that if you would believe you would see the glory of God?" Then they took away the stone from the place where the dead man was lying. And Jesus lifted up His eyes and said, "Father, I thank You that You have heard Me. And I know that You always hear Me, but because of the people who are standing by I said this, that they may believe that You sent Me."*
>
> *John 11:40-42*

While the curious bystanders were witnesses to one of the greatest recorded miracles, they could not have known that they would also be participants. By commanding *the people* to loose Lazarus – family, friends, neighbors and strangers – He was showing us all that we are to be His hands on this earth. We are to walk

The Walk

together with one another, to help one another, to loose one another from the trappings that have us bound.

This is not to say that we are responsible for anyone else's walk, or that we are to carry the baggage of those who should be carrying their own. (Remember, the people did not loose Lazarus from his graveclothes until Jesus gave the go-ahead.) The key here is to understand that this is a Christian *walk* – a journey. And, there are stretches along the way that we are to tackle together.

As the classic poem, *Footprints* reminds us, there are times when we'll be called upon to walk on our own, and times when the Lord will carry us. Likewise, there are times when we'll be asked to walk together with others – or even to loose one another from the ties that bind and hinder us from a victorious walk of resurrection life.

A Two-Way Street

It's probably a good idea for those seeking a successful Christian walk to devote a little extra time and effort to walking with others. We tend to focus our attention and effort to trying to please God, but sometimes fail to recognize the importance He places on His children walking in love together.

So, let's consider another aspect of our walk with our fellow human beings.

We must take care not to put undue burdens on ourselves to be all-loving, gracious and humble toward others – you know, the old "esteeming others higher than self" admonition. Admittedly, it's a delicate balance, and we are to treat others as *we would have them* treat us, not *as they do* treat us. But, there's still a two-way street along which we can walk together.

"that they all may be one, as You, Father, are in Me, and I in You; that they also may be one in Us, that the world may believe that You sent Me. And the glory which You gave Me I have given them, that they may be one just as We are one: I in them, and you in Me; that they may be made perfect in one, and that the world may know that You have sent Me, and have loved them as You have loved Me."

John 17:21-23

Along with the heartfelt prayer that the Lord Jesus prayed on our behalf comes responsibility. If the illustration of His relationship with the Father as an example can be summed up in one word, that word might be *balance*. Or, perhaps *symmetry* – that perfect unison and harmony that would make us the well-oiled machine God intends us to be, in one-on-one relationships, small groups, churches and communities. But, achieving such a delicate balance requires all hands on deck. Each relationship is a two-way street, and the same standards apply to us all.

Have you ever found yourself in relationship with someone who expects you to do all the work? Maybe it was a relationship you really wanted to grow, but felt that the other party didn't. You initiated all the phone calls and e-mails. Get-togethers always seemed to be at your house, or you constantly found yourself doing the cooking, cleaning, shopping or driving. It didn't work, did it? Such lopsided relationships never do. And, it doesn't take long to conclude that it's just not worth your effort.

Valuing others enough to esteem them higher than ourselves, and valuing ourselves enough to not let others walk all over us, is indeed a balancing act. To pull off this feat will mean establishing expectations and boundaries in relationships. If someone takes advantage of your good will once, whether by borrowing money, bumming a ride or forgetting a commitment, that's usually not a problem. But, when they don't repay the loan, or they continue bumming rides and forgetting commitments, then it's time to establish ground rules in the relationship. They must understand that you don't expect to be treated this way. If the shabby treatment continues, they've crossed your boundaries and violated, if not destroyed, the relationship. Of course, you must similarly honor their expectations and boundaries.

Some people will bend over backwards to do anything in their power to preserve a friendship. That's not necessarily a bad thing, but if you find yourself making all the sacrifices, it's probably time to question whether it's really a friendship at all. It's probably time to move on. There are also those who really don't know they're taking advantage. Perhaps their inconsiderate treatment of others is not intentional. This is where grace comes in. Think of the Father's long-suffering with some of our shenanigans – not only the accidental, unintentional ones, but even those antics that He's repeatedly warned and convicted us of!

One of the fun things about relationships, especially developing new ones, is the creativity we get to employ. As we've seen, we all have different gifts and talents and skill sets. If I'm a planner and list-maker, I may be called on to create the itinerary for a vacation or day excursion. Someone else who may be more creative or artistic could be asked to decorate for a party or other function. Not only are we both willing to use our gifts as a contribution to the relationship, but the gratification and fulfillment that comes with doing what we enjoy and are good at will enhance the bond all the more. No one feels used or "put-upon."

There is a custom in the southwest African country of Angola (and probably in many regions of the world, hopefully including the U.S.) whereby, if you cook a meal for someone or send a homemade dish to their home, your pot or bowl is never returned empty. They may not have much. Perhaps you'll receive a bowl full of hand-picked fruit, corn flour, or maybe just rice. But there will always be a quid pro quo of some sort. This is a classic illustration of the two-way relationship and its importance in our walk together with others.

III.

Walking With God

Knowing God

Many have read well-known literary works like The Pursuit of God by A. W. Tozer, or Knowing God by J. I. Packer -- true classics in Christendom. Most of us pored over these volumes early in our Christian walk, in an effort not only to draw near to God, but to learn how Christianity is "done."

Now that we're older and (hopefully) wiser, we've come to realize that it's not so much a learning experience as a *process* of being, doing, and growing. While we've gleaned valuable guidance from spiritual giants like Tozer and others, our relationship with God differs from theirs. And, much like a marriage, the relationship evolves as we come to know the Father better.

The Walk

Think of the many well-meaning friends and relatives who offered their sage marital advice before you tied the knot -- and how little of that advice could actually be applied to your own marriage.

Look also at your relationship with your parents, and your siblings' relationships with them. Different, aren't they? Although some may chalk it up to favoritism, the truth is, no child is going to relate to their parents in the same way as their brother or sister. How can they? If one child is happy-go-lucky and his sister is more serious and intense, their interactions with others cannot be identical.

The Lord sees each one of His children differently because He created us differently. He knows our ways, our thoughts, our joys and hurts, our likes and dislikes. He knows us *intimately.* And the key to our walk with Him is to know the same things about Him.

We have a built-in advantage in developing this walk with God: His Word. In it, He speaks pretty clearly about the things that are pleasing to Him, and even those that He hates. (Always a drag when you recognize your own ways in that latter list. Ouch!)

So, what are some of God's likes and dislikes? As we get to know Him, have we figured out whether He would be a vanilla or chocolate ice cream type? An SUV or a pick-up? Paper or plastic?

For Glory and for Beauty

Through God's Word and countless other avenues, I believe we can learn some things about Him that might not be spelled out for us. It may take some digging, but don't we invest that much effort in any relationship that we value?

I happen to think God is a lover of beauty. You know, things that are pleasing to the senses --a work of art, a musical masterpiece, a literary tour de force.

I pondered whether God indeed appreciates beauty on a visit to Italy when, surrounded by great cathedrals, the gold and marble, the breathtaking architecture, intricate sculptures, masterful paintings and frescoes, I was taken aback. As a history buff, I'd seen all the photos and studied the origins of these great works. I thought I knew what to expect. But I wasn't prepared. The grandeur of it all quickly turned my smugness to awe.

But after recovering from the shock of seeing the great works in person, I began to stew about it. I kept coming back to one question: Why?

I had always taken a dim view of the extravagance and lavishness that mark some of our better-known historical sites and attractions. The Vatican and its surroundings were a particular enigma for me. While I knew there were many monuments and great wonders that were constructed for practical purposes, such as the Great Wall, and others conceived and erected as a symbol of love (the Taj Mahal and the Hanging Gardens), what was the purpose of the spare-no-expense attitude of the papacy?

To my mind, there was only one correct answer: There was no good purpose, certainly none that was pleasing to God. All the over-the-top opulence was simply intended to symbolize holiness in Popes and priests, a holiness that is only rightfully attributable to God Himself.

Well, the Holy Spirit quickly took me to task over this attitude.

Have you ever noticed how protective and defensive we tend to get when it comes to God? As if we're His appointed bodyguards, or we're His advocate rather than He ours. We become dutifully indignant when we hear someone blaspheming His name or trying to steal His thunder (because, of course, we would never commit such atrocities). Well, that's all fine, but maybe it's time we came down from our high horses and gave some consideration to what God really thinks. Could it be that we really don't even know Him well enough to defend Him?

Now, we do know that we are to have no other gods before Him – no idols are to be worshipped and no relationships held in higher esteem than the one we enjoy with Him. We're not to stand around gawking in awe at things. But, you have to admit, there are some pretty awesome things all around us. Granted, most are things that God created – the mountains, the ocean, sunsets, flowers, animals, and so on. He is pleased and glorified when we ogle at these masterpieces. But what about the manmade stuff – particularly if those things were created by unbelievers, with no thought of bringing glory to God at all?

I believe the answer can be found in the very holiness and majesty of the Father Himself. And, because He has made everything beautiful in its time (Ecc. 3:11) and all things were made through Him, and without Him nothing was made that was made (John 1:3), it is clear that He not only appreciates beauty, but His fingerprint is on all that we see around us today. Artistic skills and talents are just some of the many gifts we have of Him and, when used to produce masterful, historic works, they will bring Him glory – whether intended or not.

While examining such works in Italy, I came to realize that the grandeur of the churches, sculptures, monuments and museums points directly to the work of Almighty God in the willing vessels of men.

In the book of Exodus, as God gave Moses instructions for the temple and the priestly garments, He also offered an explicit purpose for the precious metals and stones, the scarlet and linen and the intricate designs: for glory and for beauty.

> *And you shall make holy garments for Aaron your brother, for glory and for beauty. So you shall speak to all who are gifted artisans, whom I have filled with the spirit of wisdom, that they may make Aaron's garments, to consecrate him, that he may minister to Me as priest.*
> Ex. 28:2-3

Several times throughout Exodus 26, 27 and 28, we find the words "ornamental," "artistically worked," and "skillfully woven." In other words, none of it was an accident. God clearly said that He would fill the artisans with a spirit of wisdom, for the express purpose of producing beauty and master craftsmanship. And, while the children of Israel were God's chosen people, and the end result of these works would be to glorify their Lord, the fact remains that He is indeed pleased by beauty in and of itself. Why? Because it is He who has filled man with the spirit that creates it.

The Walk

I've long been a fan of Michelangelo. Upon a reading of The Agony and the Ecstasy, or a conversation with a knowledgeable tour guide in Florence or Rome, we learn much about this most gifted Renaissance artist, and the inexplicable gift he was given. Of the amazing sculpture La Pieta, there were complaints that the face of Mary was too youthful as the lifeless body of her crucified 33-year-old Son lay across her lap. Michelangelo defended his decision, insisting he would always portray Mary as pure and innocent, notwithstanding his critics. In the commanding, historic David the King, he aimed to portray youthfulness yet power, winsomeness yet authority. In his sculpture of Moses, one profile depicts the wonder of having been on the mountain with the Lord for forty days and nights, and the opposite profile shouts his dismay and anger at what he found when he came down from the mountain – all within the same life-sized figure, carved from one solid block of marble.

This is the "artistically worked" beauty of which the Scriptures speak. And then there's the ceiling of the Sistine Chapel -- an unbelievable accomplishment considering that Michelangelo was a sculptor, not a painter. He was commissioned (ordered) to paint the ceiling, but readily confessed that he never wanted to!

As I toured the landmarks and marvelous works of Italy, I listened and observed the reactions of my fellow tourists. Of course, all were impressed. But I was fascinated to hear the comments of those who were clearly not believers and had little or no prior knowledge of the works or their history. Young and old alike, from every corner of the globe, listened intently as our tour guide freely and openly discussed biblical history and characters. Most seemed to look with new eyes, full of reverence and awe. And God was glorified.

In His Image

Have you ever considered that, because we are made in the image of God, it is no accident that we rejoice in beauty? That we admire strength, courage and honor? Or, that we empathize with and feel the pain of others? It's hereditary! These are attributes of our Father, the same traits that He appreciates.

Understanding the things that God appreciates, and those that are meaningful to Him, are a fundamental part of knowing Him. We often assume that our relationship with the Father is simply a matter of obeying His Word. But there are more "layers" to Him than that. Yes, He wants obedience, not only for His glory, but for our own good. Likewise, He wants us to enjoy the beauty of His creation, as well as the God-given gift of creating with our own hands -- both for His enjoyment and our own.

My pastor recently discussed how much God cares for us -- not only loves us and desires to use us, but genuinely cares for our happiness and well-being. In Genesis 15, we find Abram a little down and despondent, despite his great victory in rescuing his nephew Lot from captivity. Although God has assured Abram that He is his shield, his exceedingly great reward, Abram is still concerned over his lack of a child and an heir. He wonders aloud to God whether his Damascan servant is to be his heir. The Lord could have simply said, "Trust Me," but He chose instead to encourage Abram by revealing His plan:

> *And behold, the word of the Lord came to him, saying, "This one shall not be your heir, but one who will come from your own body shall be your heir." Then He brought him outside and said, "Look now toward heaven, and count the stars if you are able to number them." And He said to him, "So shall your descendants be."*
>
> Gen. 15:4-5

God indeed cares about beauty, but not only the physical, tangible, material stuff. He desires that our very souls be filled with the beauty of the knowledge of Him, the peace, hope, joy and rest we have in Him. They are attributes of His character and, consequently, they are to be ours as His children. These are also important elements in our walk with God, and not for His glory alone, but for our own good.

Ultimate Beauty

Consider heaven and hell. The latter is thought to be dark and menacing, with the only light likely being the raging fire that consumes its inhabitants eternally. Heaven, in contrast, promises a

The Walk

sparkling "sea of glass;" precious stones of size and perfection beyond what we can imagine; and, the glorious light of the Lamb of God providing illumination like nothing before seen.

Growing in our walk with God will require growing in our knowledge of Him. And, although it may require a little extra digging – perhaps in study, meditation and prayer -- it's not as difficult as we might think. Sometimes it's just a matter of common sense -- or, maybe a glance in the mirror, if we can see past the worldly junk to the beautiful image in which we were created.

The Measure of a Man

One of the most difficult challenges to overcome in this Christian walk is the notion that we are products of our environment. Heaven may be our home, but we're journeying through a fallen world. We ourselves may be spirit, but we're housed in this nagging flesh.

Whether we like it or not (and, even if we refuse to admit it), our environment has a powerful influence on us. We measure people and things based on faulty criteria like emotions or negative experiences. We even measure God with those worldly yardsticks.

How often have you heard someone give praise to God *because* He did this or that for them? I used to do it all the time. Until the day came when I realized what I

The Walk

was doing, and how it was hindering my walk with God.

The morning air was clean, and the midsummer Louisiana sun had yet to become oppressive. As I settled into a comfortable chair on our deck, my heart overflowed with joy and thanksgiving.

I had just spent some time rehearsing how I would later tell my girlfriends about the ways I'd seen the Lord's goodness to me that week. Then, we would "worship" Him together. That was how we did things. Whenever we felt especially blessed in some way, or just had a particularly nice day, we'd call one another and praise God "because . . ."

Now, delighting in the weather and the absence of allergies, I began to worship God accordingly.

Wait a minute. *Accordingly?* What was wrong with this picture?

There in my deck chair, the Spirit of God exposed the flawed, self-centered exercise I'd so often thought of as worship. It was as if I was trying to reward God for bringing good things to my life and, by withholding praise, to punish Him for allowing the bad. I couldn't recall offering many praises during bad times. Where had I stumbled into behaving as if God was worthy of honor only when I got my way or received sufficient blessings?

Over the next few weeks, my motives for worship began to change. I slowly came to understand the words to a song I'd often sung: "It's all about You, Lord." God's worthiness of worship had nothing at all to do with me or my vaporous existence. It simply wasn't about my experiences, environment or emotions.

Taming the Environment

There are ways around the environmental trap that will enable us have our walk with God spill over into our everyday routine, rather than vice versa.

But first, there's a caveat that shouldn't be overlooked: Getting to that place will take some doing. We still live in a fallen world, and our spirits are still covered in sinful flesh. There will still be traffic, bills, sickness and co-workers, and we'll still react to them in wrong ways. We'll be angry and grouchy, we'll pout and sulk and gossip and complain. And, we'll neglect to give praise to God -- that is, until the next time we feel sufficiently "blessed."

Possibly the most important thing to remember in our attitude adjustment is that we are walking *with* God. (In fact, if we're smart, we'll get in lockstep with Him!) That means He's right there on the path with us. None of what we're going through is foreign or unknown to Him, even if our emotions tell us we're out on a limb all alone.

In the book of Ruth we find Naomi, a Hebrew woman who had gone with her husband and sons to live in Moab due to a famine in their Bethlehem home. But her husband and sons died in Moab, leaving Naomi in a foreign land with her Moabite daughters-in-law.

At this point, the story is disheartening to say the least. Of course, it does get better, after Naomi returns to Bethlehem with her daughter-in-law Ruth. But, in the process, it is Naomi's fluctuating attitudes that are of note.

> *... for it grieves me very much for your sakes that the hand of*

the Lord has gone out against me!

Do not call me Naomi; call me Mara, for the Almighty has dealt very bitterly with me. I went out full, and the Lord has brought me home again empty. Why do you call me Naomi, since the Lord has testified against me, and the Almighty has afflicted me?
Ruth 1:13b, 20-21

There is no doubt that Naomi's circumstances were grim, and the future looked bleak. But, by blaming the Lord for her troubles, she was carrying the pity party a bit far. Nowhere in the first chapter of Ruth is there any record of Naomi praising the Lord, or even seeking Him in her dire situation. She clearly did not believe that the Lord was walking *with* her through the storm. It sounds as if she may not have believed at that time that He was available to her at all.

Even after Naomi returned to her own people in Bethlehem, she wasn't thankful. But, note the change in attitude when her *circumstances* began to change:

The Walk

> *Then Naomi said to her daughter-in-law, "Blessed be he of the Lord, who has not forsaken His kindness to the living and the dead!"*
> *Ruth 2:20a*

God had a plan for Naomi and for her daughter-in-law, Ruth. That plan had been formulated before the two women were ever conceived. And none of their ups or downs, successes or failures, trials or mountaintop experiences were going to change God's plan. Only their *attitudes* could delay His blessing or postpone their joy. Naomi had a choice, as do we in each of our present-day circumstances. She chose to measure God's goodness by her circumstances, and to embrace her misery until she *saw* better days. The wise choice would have been to praise the Lord notwithstanding the circumstances – simply because He is worthy – and to trust that there would be better days ahead.

It's not a fun lesson to learn, and not an easy one. But, I've tried to learn it well. On that long-ago Louisiana morning, I embarked upon a journey that continues today -- discovering the joy of glorying only in the Lord (1 Cor. 1:31). In the process, I've developed new worship habits.

I try to spend at least a few moments each day setting my mind on God's holiness, His awesome power, His tender love, His glorious creation. To do so, I meditate on Scripture that describes Him, such as Is. 6:1–5.

I look for lyrics that keep my focus upon God alone (rather than those that speak of what He has done or will do for me). Singing these songs aloud to the Lord helps me to remember the object of my worship.

Using the Lord's Prayer in Matthew 6 as my guide, I begin my prayers by hallowing God's name.

Sometimes, if I'm anxious about a particular need for which I'm praying, I turn away from that petition and praise God instead. When I return to my prayer request, I acknowledge that every good thing in my life is from Him (James 1:17). Of course, we are always welcome to come boldly to His throne of grace with our petitions (Heb. 4:16). But for the purpose of learning to separate my needs from His worthiness, I've had to be very intentional.

I'm learning to see my conversations with my friends differently. We used to act as if liberally sprinkling "Praise God!" throughout our conversations constituted honoring and worshiping Him. Together, however, we've discovered that worship requires us to give God the honor He is due – apart from our prayer requests or perceptions of His blessings in our lives.

What the Lord began to teach me about worship that day on my deck is not a legalistic ritual that fits neatly into a particular compartment of my life. Rather, it is a joyous and liberating practice that allows me to seek Him with my whole heart and to know Him better – no matter the circumstances of the day.

Be Still and Know

It's hard to be still these days. It just doesn't seem to come naturally. We have to "purpose in our hearts" and "set our minds," and all that good stuff. But, why?

Never before in our society (or any other society that I know of) has life been so busy. What little free time we have is often spent reading self-help books on how to find more free time. And we're all exhausted. Something's wrong with this picture.

The interesting thing is, being still is something that should come naturally to us, because we were created that way.

> *And they heard the sound of the Lord God walking in the*

The Walk

garden in the cool of the day...
Genesis 3:8a

As Charles Stanley says of this passage in his Life Principles Bible, "God created us to interact with Him in an intimate friendship, even on a face-to-face basis. God desires that we walk with Him daily, enjoying the rich fellowship that He offers."

Such rich, intimate fellowship cannot be accomplished without being still. Even being about the Lord's business in work, ministry and family life naturally requires rest. In fact, I have a theory that Christian rest equals Christian growth. Sounds oxymoronic, doesn't it?

It sort of stands to reason that, in order to grow, one must work harder, faster, longer; one must compete, strive, strategize. And, in order make progress in our walk, some believe there is just no time to be still. That theory certainly has its place.

When I think of marathon-type races such as the Tour de France or the Iditarod, it is interesting to note how the participants all take the full measure of rest time allotted to them. Though adrenaline is pumping and they may feel well able to go another so many miles without a break, wisdom instructs them otherwise. If they listen to their flesh at such a critical point, they will be deceived. Even auto racers and their teams must carefully weigh the risk of foregoing a pit stop in order to gain a few more laps.

The Christian walk must be that of a marathoner, not a sprinter. We're in this thing for the long haul. There must be a steady pace, a determined consistency, a sure stride. Adherence to the rules is a must; integrity and dependability are required. And, that all-important word, *balance,* is key.

> *There remains therefore a rest for the people of God. For he who has entered His rest has himself also ceased from his works as God did from His.*
> *Hebrews 4:9-10*

Personally, I find life today not only way too busy, but unbearably noisy. Somehow, when I picture God walking in the garden with Adam and Eve in the

The Walk

cool of the day, I don't envision the hum of appliances, the blare of car horns or the inane babble of the television as part of the background ambiance. Being still before God is a crucial element of our walk with Him, and times of silence are an important part of being still.

I've heard it said that when God has a hard time getting us to be still and listen, He will create circumstances that force our stillness and quietness before Him. That may or may not be true. While there is indeed a stillness that is borne of circumstantial necessity such as illness, that stillness may not involve listening at all, but simply waiting anxiously to be on the go again. This type of stillness is rarely fruitful. The stillness that is required in our walk with God includes seeking His face and listening attentively to His voice. Several years ago, I learned in a most dramatic way what this stillness looks like.

My third bout with malaria came several years into my tenure on the mission field. It was at a time when the war in Angola was heating up, with rebel attacks and skirmishes moving closer to our village, making ingress and egress more and more difficult for several weeks. My team and I weren't too concerned since we had plenty of supplies and no real need to travel.

When the fever and chills began to set in, I knew it was malaria, but I was out of quinine to treat it. A friend who was a former paramedic and sold various drugs at the outdoor marketplace gave me a new medication that UNICEF had just brought into the country. I took the suggested dosage at about 7 p.m. and took to my bed. I must have fallen asleep instantly.

The banging on the door seemed miles away, and I struggled to forge past the grogginess. It was a surreal feeling. I was so dizzy, and nauseous. My head was swimming. I heard voices in the distance. Claudio, a friend who helped with some of our Bible studies, was talking to some other team members. Their voices sounded to me like 45 rpm records being played on a 33 rpm setting. What was wrong with me? Why couldn't I wake up?

There was a knock at my bedroom door. *It's UNITA,* came the dire pronouncement. UNITA was the brutal rebel group that had already wreaked havoc throughout the country, causing the civil

The Walk

war to drag on for years. And now, they were attacking our village. It was 10 p.m. and our friends and neighbors crowded onto the road, fleeing the area on foot with their meager belongings stacked on their heads.

Through the fog that was my mind, I tried to process the information. I was still lying in bed, as my concerned friends' heads began to poke through the door. I explained my symptoms and between us we were able to identify the problem – vertigo! It had to be a reaction to the new medication. It was as if the room was spinning in one direction and my head was spinning in the opposite direction. So long as I focused on one spot, I was okay. But if I tried to move my head, or even shift my eyes, the sickening spinning would return. I had to remain perfectly still. With a raging fever, I couldn't even wipe the sweat from my face.

Everything was happening so fast, and there were so many variables to consider. My greatest concern was for the two young orphaned boys who were staying at our compound, sleeping soundly in the next room. How close was the rebel force? Would we have to flee? What would we take with us? My two team members decided to run down to the village chief's residence to see what they could learn. *"Carla, we'll be right back. Don't open the door for anyone, and don't try to move."* (Like that was gonna happen.)

I lay there with my eyes closed, half-praying and half-scheming. *Let's see, if anyone tries to come into the house, I'll just take the boys and we'll head out the back door. We can hide in the ditch and cover up with banana leaves...* Wait a minute! I wasn't going anywhere! I couldn't move!

My plans melted into the most passionate of silent prayers. I knew what we were facing. The others might never return. The boys and I were sitting ducks. Enter the Lord.

> *You will not have to fight this battle. Take your position; stand still and see the deliverance the Lord will give you.*
> 2 Chron. 20:17

Suddenly a wave of peace flooded over me. I knew God was speaking. I knew

The Walk

that in the stillness of the moment, I needed to do nothing at all. The position I was to take was one of stillness. I was to simply rest. Anxiety left me. There was no need to plan, try or even hope to take any action. This was the type of stillness to which the Lord had been calling me. This was pure rest, and it had miraculously been found in the midst of the most perilous circumstances.

The guys did indeed return, with the decision not to try to leave. Yes, it would be dangerous to stay, but it would be just as risky to join the hundreds of people venturing out into the night. We would hold a prayer vigil through the night, and the Lord would deliver us.

It was to be 36 hours before we felt safe going out. My symptoms began to dissipate, villagers were trickling back, and the grim toll from the attack began to circulate. There had been several killings, mostly on the outskirts of the village. One of Claudio's best friends was among them. The experience had been horrendous for us all, but the resulting lessons would not have been learned under lesser circumstances.

Perhaps the moral of the story is this: Our first goal should be that such extreme situations in our lives will not to be necessary in order to get us to be still before the Lord. But, should we find ourselves in such a valley, we must take care to make good use of our time there – not e-mailing, texting, planning or scheming; not complaining, questioning or doubting. Simply being still. And listening for the still, small voice that will lead us out of that miry clay and back onto the path that is bathed in His marvelous light.

The Walk

The complexities of our walk with self and with others can be narrowed down to a single theme: Esteem others higher, or better, than yourself (Phil. 2:3). After all, that's what the whole J-O-Y concept is all about. But, as we've seen, although it sounds simple enough, it is not. And God didn't intend it to be.

Have you ever wondered why the Christian life is even called a "walk?" It's a pretty provocative proposition when you think about it. All sorts of questions are conjured up: Where are we going? How do we get there? Will we have a map? GPS? Why doesn't God just fly us in?

Years ago, there was a participant in the New York and Boston Marathons named Rosie Ruiz. In New York, she completed

The Walk

the race in a respectable time, qualifying her to compete in Boston. There, she crossed the finish line ahead of all other female runners, and everyone was amazed at her winning time. But, before long there were whispers and murmurings. Those who knew about such things wondered at the lack of sweat and salt deposits on her skin after both contests. She just didn't *look* as if she'd run 26 miles.

Turns out, Rosie took the subway. That's right. She started the race in New York with everyone else, then hopped on the subway, re-entering the marathon fresh as a daisy during the last half-mile. She repeated the fraud in Boston but, days after being crowned the victor, her fraud was exposed and she was stripped of her title and her winnings.

Ruiz used deception to avoid the rigors of training for a tough challenge, and then walking – or running – it out. She was neither prepared to deal with self nor with her fellow runners. In the marathon that is our Christian walk, there can be no such escape. Try as we might, we won't fool God into giving us a free pass. He insists that we hunker down with Him to train and prepare for our journey.

Carla Bastos

Training for a competition is tough by any measure, because it involves so much time alone with our self-discipline, or lack of same. But then, when it's time to compete, we have to face others, as teammates, opponents, or both. And, of course, everybody's got a different idea of how things should be done. It just complicates the journey even more. In times like these, how often have you wondered, *Why can't others just think like I do?* (Come on, 'fess up – you have those moments, too. You know, those times when we wish everyone else would just accept that our way is the best way. Life would be so much easier!)

That's exactly why we don't get that one-way, first-class ticket to our destination. We are sojourners. We're on a journey, and the goal is not comfort and ease. Taking a journey is not the same as taking a trip. It's not a jam-packed week of fun and indulgence. We stop, we explore, we learn, we grow. We stumble and fall, we skin our knees and pout and whine periodically. There will be long stretches of grueling uphill climbs – balanced by times of rest and refreshing, and even fun and indulgence. There are dangers, to be sure – hitchhikers,

The Walk

hijackers and bad drivers who seem to want to run over us; downpours and potholes, searing heat, whipping winds and weariness are also part of the mix.

But, through it all, we do get a roadmap and, even better than a GPS, we have a live Guide to show us the way. And, by the way, our shoes will never wear out.

When we get to the end of the road, we'll have a better understanding of self and, lo and behold, we'll find that our way wasn't the best way after all. We'll have precious, rich relationships with folks to whom we didn't want to give the time of day. We'll be stronger and healthier, physically, mentally, emotionally and spiritually, because we walked it out instead of phoning it in (or taking the subway!) And, we'll know that the journey was not only necessary, but worth every step.

A Walk with the Master

We've seen the importance of making straight paths for ourselves. But, Scripture also admonishes us to make straight paths for our Lord. John the Baptist employed the exhortation of the prophet Isaiah in illustrating the process of our walk with God.

> *Prepare the way of the Lord; make straight in the desert a highway for our God. Every valley shall be exalted, and every mountain and hill shall be made low; the crooked places shall be made straight, and the rough places smooth; the glory of the Lord shall be revealed, and all flesh shall see it together; for the mouth of the Lord has spoken.*
> *Isaiah 40:3-6*

It's a little daunting to imagine how pristine a road must be in order for Almighty God to walk on it. But, keep in mind, all we're required to do is *prepare* the way. Once our hearts are ready to receive Him, through daily confession and repentance, then *He* will see that the valleys are exalted and the mountains and hills made low; it is *He* who will make the crooked places straight, and the rough places smooth. And His glory will be revealed.

The Walk

This is the Way

Although the Lord allows our walk to be difficult enough to challenge and grow us, He never leaves us along the way. When we veer off onto dangerous or uncharted roads, whether out of rebellion or ignorance, He is faithful in His grace to put us back on course. He patiently waits for us to come to our senses.

> *Therefore the Lord will wait, that He may be gracious to you; and therefore He will be exalted, that He may have mercy on you. For the Lord is a God of justice; blessed are all those who wait for Him.*
>
> *And though the Lord gives you the bread of adversity and the water of affliction, yet your teachers will not be moved into a corner anymore, but your eyes shall see your teachers.*
>
> *Your ears shall hear a word behind you, saying "This is the way, walk in it," whenever you turn to the right hand or whenever you turn to the left.*
> *Isaiah 30:18, 20-21*

God is not trying to hide His will from us, and He doesn't want to see us stumble down the wrong path. He is waiting for us to seek His face, to desire His will. And then He not only shows us the correct path, but He lights it for us.

There is one caveat here, though. If you hear a word *behind* you telling you the way, something is wrong with this picture.

These prophecies from Isaiah were given at a time of rebellion among the children of Israel, despite repeated warnings from the Lord:

> *For thus says the Lord God, the Holy One of Israel: In returning and rest you shall be saved; in quietness and confidence shall be your strength." But you would not, and you said, "No, for we will flee on horses. Therefore, you shall flee! And, "We will ride on swift horses." Therefore those who pursue you shall be swift!*
> *Isaiah 30:15-16*

The Walk

Because of the rebellion of His children, the Lord was forced to give them over to their enemies. He wouldn't continue to protect them when they wouldn't even acknowledge Him as their Protector.

No doubt we've all been amazed at times at the insolence of the children of Israel. Their walk over hundreds of years was a vicious cycle: First obedience; then rebellion; then judges and prophets brought conviction and pronounced chastisement; then repentance and forgiveness; and then, back to square one to start the whole process again. This is exactly why they spent forty years in the wilderness to make an eleven-day journey!

The truth is, our walk is no different from theirs. We get sloppy and lazy, or we go off on our own to "explore" a little. And, before we know it, the voice of our Guide is coming from behind us. We're no longer following, but attempting to show God the way – our way.

I've been with tour groups in foreign lands and, inevitably, one person or couple will wander off. Their curiosity may get the better of them, or they just don't have the patience to wait for the stragglers. These impatient ones will often get separated from the group, sometimes even getting lost altogether. And, in a sort of poetic justice, the rest of the group will have to wait *for them* to be found.

There are certainly wonderful sights to see, lessons to learn and people to meet along our Walk. The Lord doesn't want us to miss out on any of it. But, although He doesn't frown on adventurous types, He wants us to remember one important thing: *The Guide knows the way!*

Walking hand-in-hand with the Creator of the universe can be a tad intimidating if we allow ourselves to over-think it. After all, we know we'll never measure up. We'll never be as holy, as loving or as righteous as we may strive to be. The trick is to place our hand *in* His. We may be walking with Him, but He alone must be leading the way. He alone is all-holy, all-loving, all-righteous. And He alone loves us enough to invite us to come along with Him on The Walk.

Until we reach the end of the road...

www.ingramcontent.com/pod-product-compliance
Lightning Source LLC
Chambersburg PA
CBHW061454040426
42450CB00007B/1360